A Quintet for Dawn

Books by Maik Nwosu

Novels
Invisible Chapters
Alpha Song
A Gecko's Farewell
The Book of Everything

Poetry
Suns of Kush
Stanzas from the Underground

Short Stories
Return to Algadez

Drama
A Quintet for Dawn

A Quintet for Dawn
by
Maik Nwosu

CROSSROADS
New York, 2025

Published by
CROSSROADS
1178 Broadway
3rd Floor, #1333
New York, NY 10001

© 2025 by Maik Nwosu. All rights reserved.
Printed in the United States of America
Cover art: Victor Ekpuk

This is a work of fiction. All names, characters, places, and incidents are products of the author's imagination or are used fictitiously.

ISBN 979-8-9904712-4-5

Characters

Narrator/Doctor
Patient/Lele
Farida
Adaeze
Abdallah

Only one part of the stage is lit: a psychiatrist's consulting room – that is, an entrance door, a couch, a chair beside it, a mirror facing the couch at a right angle, a large painting of fists on the wall beside the door. On the unlit part of the stage: a totem in the foreground and a lamppost in the background. When the curtain rises, the Narrator/Doctor, dressed in a doctor's overall, is already in the consulting room.

Narrator: "Hallelujah!" That was the first word he uttered the day he burst into my consulting room. "Hallelujah?" I asked. "Hallelujah! Hallelujah!" he chanted emphatically. I knew his type, or so I thought. "Jesus is coming soon, eh?" I inquired with a conspiratorial wink. I was in an upbeat mood, and I had no patient to attend to at the time. "Don't you understand?" he asked with a frown on his face. "I am Hallelujah Y, the incomplete revelation. All incomplete revelations carry in their genes an enlarging Y factor – unclear, unknown, and perhaps unknowable." I wasn't sure about his type anymore, but I immediately liked the sound of him. I was compiling my case studies at the time, and I immediately wanted to include him. I wanted his apparent latitude. So, I invited him to lie back on the couch and we began. No appointment, no wait, no fee. There is no doubt about it: D.B. Lele, Journalist with a Wildfire Reputation, had a certain affective aura. For six days, he took me on a maze of a journey. It was not until the seventh day that I finally got to the bottom of the matter, so to speak.

A knock on the door. It is opened from the outside and the Patient enters. He and the Narrator/Doctor exchange greetings before the Doctor leads him to the forestage adjacent to the couch.

Narrator: As usual, we started with muscular activity. We started with press-ups. The count was mine. "1...yes, 2...yes, 3...yes, 4...yes, 5...yes. Changing count now, changing count! Up...down, up...down, up...down, up...down, up...down. Time to relax now, time!"

The two men stretch themselves.

Patient: What a morning! I think you should adjust your signpost to read: Dr. A. C. Ilo, Psychiatrist AND body trainer.
Doctor (with a laugh): And your card should read: Mr. D.B. Lele, journalist AND complainant. The press-ups are for my VIPs: Very Important Patients. Nothing like press-ups to relax the body and the mind.
Patient (mimicking the doctor): 1...yes, 2...yes, 3...
Doctor: Yes.
Patient: Yes?
Doctor: Yes.
Patient: And that yeses the mind into relaxation?
Doctor: Every each time. Every each time. Now, we begin. Why don't you lie back nicely...
Patient (lying back on the couch): Done, as requested. VIP Obeys VIP. Not a bad headline, is it?
Doctor (sitting in his chair): What other VIP?
Patient: Very Important Psychiatrist.

Joint laughter.

Patient (again mimicking the doctor): Up...down, up...down, up...down... The rhythm of the world. Reminds me of my upstairs neighbor and his wife. Every each night, to adapt your favorite expression, they are at it. "Le le," grunts the man every time he descends; "Le Le," moans the wife. Quite a concert, I tell you. And there I lie in my bachelor apartment below wondering at this ritual during which my name is scissored every night. When they finally peak, then and only then does the synthesis occur – with orgasmic ecstasy, I suppose: "Le le! Le le!" They go on and on. Every each night.
Doctor: And how does that make you feel?
Patient: I start with an erection and end with an orgasm, sometimes. Every each night, I partake in that carnal communion from my

downstairs apartment. And it's cheap at the price of a dismembered name, which in any case is at last conjoined in equal proportion.

Doctor: Cheap, certainly. Satisfying?

Patient (impatiently): An orgasm is an orgasm, doctor.

Doctor: You are attracted to her, aren't you?

Patient: I have never truly seen her. The very few times she leaves the apartment, she goes out wearing a gown with only a pair of slits to allow the eyes a narrowed view of the world. Sometimes, she appears as lean as the afternoon haze. At other times, she seems full like the evening shade. I suppose it is a varying trick of the gown. And because I have never truly seen her, my imagination can recreate her limitlessly. Some nights her voice comes to me dry as the desert wind, then she is taut and dry and I have to work harder at it. On other nights, her voice comes full and sensuous and then she is wanton and wet. Those nights, doctor, O Lord 1-2-3-yes...those nights!

Doctor: And the man?

Patient (with a sigh): The poor fellow exudes a mousy contentment, but I've also seen him dart into brothels. It's hard not to be bored with the same woman every each night. The poor fellow! Me, I get all the variety I want without leaving my bedroom.

Doctor: Quite interesting. Very very interesting. Have you read Freud?

Patient (emphatically): Freud is dead!

Doctor: Oh, come on. His ideas...

Patient (in a chant): Ninja. Barawo. Ashawo. Ole. Banza. Ekpenta. Kwashiorkor.

Doctor: I see-e. Jung?

Patient (emphatically): Dead!

Doctor: But the quintessential Jung...

Patient (in a drawl): I heard them still singing, the cherubic mongrels, that London bridge is falling down, and man finally invents himself at Olduvai, even the pudgy women who fry beancakes beside refuse mountains they too have chamber stories to tell...

Doctor: All right, a-l-l r-i-g-h-t. Aristotle?

Patient: Murdered in Athens. Drank one cup too much of hemlock.

Doctor: Plato?
Patient: Platini.
Doctor: Nietzsche?
Patient: Died and resurrected in Auschwitz and Hiroshima.
Doctor (wonderingly): In Auschwitz? In Hiroshima?
Patient (impatiently): Dust to dust, ashes to ashes.
Doctor: Descartes?
Patient: On the run. A thousand bounty hunters are after him.
Doctor: Zeno?
Patient: Wanted, paradox by paradox.
Doctor: Confucius?
Patient: Confused.
Doctor: Doctor Faustus?
Patient: Quote. "Time was, Mephistopheles, your phantom medusas." Unquote. D.B. Lele.
Doctor (slowly): D.B. Lele?
Patient (with passion): He will live forever. 1-2-3 yes, forever!
Doctor: And when is the end of "forever"?
Patient: The Promised Year, when the sewage will turn into tap water and toilet paper into pounds sterling and Africa will become the center of the world. Hallelujah! The Year of All Things, when your Sigmund Yung and your Carl Freud will be exhumed and their contentious certitude exorcized in...in the cities of the posterior.
Doctor: Sigmund Yung? Carl Freud? Why the mismatch?
Patient: I won't be drawn into a dissertation on a Downstairs Orgasm Complex.
Doctor: Clarity begets wholeness.
Patient (energetically): Clarity is questionable. I should know, doctor. I've played all the roles in and out of whatever book –
fisher of men, fisher for men, kingfish, fish-king.

He begins a song. The clanging of a church bell is heard in the background as the lights dim.

When you come to collect your people

> Remember me, O Lord
> Remember me, O Lord
> When you come to collect your people
> Remember me, O Lord, Amen.

Patient: I have preached from tall pulpits the bland mercy of God and the apocalyptic joy of salvation, sometimes speaking in innumerable, undecipherable tongues.
(Rapidly):
Kataboomkataboomkatasatalamatabananalassalassalasimsamantabiri kosikabalasosososososommachasachasichasouubukataboom.
(Normally):
"Remember me, O Lord." I have heard that song sung in forlorn prison yards as plaintive supplications issuing from the tongues of forgotten Cains and Abels. And I have ministered unto them: "Remember, O people of God, that our Lord promised: 'Whenever and wherever two or three of you are gathered in My name, there I shall be.' Fear not. The Lord is with you. He will certainly not forget you on the Day of the Rapture.

Lights brighten.

Patient: Religion? I have been there. Hallelujah! It mattered not that I was kicked out of the seminary – in my penultimate year.
Doctor: You were?
Patient: Yes, I was. Because I asked an...an unanswerable question, or so it seemed.
Doctor: May I hear it?
Patient: I asked the rector what became of the Old Testament God. He contemplated me for an eternity and then he said (in a fatherly voice): "My child, God is as was and as ever shall be." "But the God of the Old Testament was the God of thunderbolts, of instant judgments," I said. "How come that God appears to have become more silent and withdrawn as the world has become more evil and soulless? Can we not infer, therefore, that it is man who has created,

or recreated, God – in his own image?" Pandemonium, doctor, p-a-n-d-e-m-o-n-i-u-m! The next day, they convened a grand inquisition.

The clanging of church bells in the background as the lights dim.

Patient: I stood in front of them in the dreaded Hall of Questions – a pitiful dot before five aged Keepers of the Gate. With great trepidation, I did their bidding. I repeated my question to the rector. "My child," he said, "is it that you do not know about the New Covenant through Christ or is it that you do not believe?" That heresy moved me to tears. I fell on my knees, with tears streaming down my face, and I tore my hair as I remonstrated with them: "But, sirs, dear sirs, is it that you do not realize that you are ascribing afterthought to a God who Himself said He never changes?" I believe I saw pity and something else on their faces as they fled from that cavernous Hall of Questions.

Lights brighten.

Patient: The next day, I was kicked out – with a question mark on my sanity. And I went on... I went on to bolder things.
Doctor: Like what?
Patient: Evangelism – of sorts, of sorts. I went on to fight in the Great War. Remember?

He begins a song. The booming of guns is heard in the background as the lights dim.

> O my home, O my home
> O my home, O my home
> When shall I see my native land?
> I'll never forget my home
>
> O my father, don't you worry
> O my mother, don't you worry

> If I happen to die in the battlefront
> Never mind
> We shall meet again

Patient: Those were the songs of the trenches, doctor, of the poor, heroic battlefields crowded with the dead and the mangled. Those were the songs of the poor cassava soldiers when the blood ran hot and the difference between the living and the dead became as tenuous as gun smoke. War? I have been there. Hallelujah! We went in with our heads and we came out with our tails, but some of us came out somewhat as vociferous as we had gone in (with vigor): "This land is ours too!"

Lights brighten.

Patient: But nothing is as was as never shall be certain. I tell you, doctor, clarity is questionable. Certainty is not of this world.
Doctor: Even in love?
Patient (passionately): Yes sir, 1-2-3, yes-yes-yes! Love? Yes, sir, I have been there. Hallelujah! But love is a joyous illiterate. That much is certain, clear.
Doctor: There is clarity in love?
Patient: In love and in looove, yes – a certain kind of clarity. Helen of Troy: The face that munched a thousand ships.
Doctor: Nefertiti of Egypt?
Patient: The Neckile.
Doctor: Imaguero of Benin?
Patient (with a chuckle): And the oba said to her: "Oba atokpe: Long live the king! I come to you with a terrible hard-on, the curse of kings. My kingdom for a cure."
Doctor: Eva Peron?
Patient (sings): "Don't cry for me, Argentina."
Doctor: Indira Gandhi?
Patient: O-o-m India, Au-u-m! Love is in infinity.
Doctor: You're a cynic with a dry sense of humor.

Patient (with vigor): All lives are lived in parenthesis. But I want expansion, doctor, illumination! Why should things, all things, not be reinvented beyond their common dimensions? Every dawn is rooted in dreams, then powered by praxis. And it's been so since the first dinosaurs came out of the water and became birds. That's the legend of dawn.

Doctor (slowly): "Since the first dinosaurs came out of the water and became birds." You sound as if you were there, as if such a thing actually happened.

Patient: Oh, I was. And it did. I'm in history, and history is in me. At the crossroads, history becomes legend and legend transcends myth.

Doctor: Crossroads?

Patient (almost without pause): What is history if not versions of memory? RSV.

Doctor: RSV?

Patient: Revised Standard Version. When you've seen it all, been it all, doctor, it's more difficult to get excited. I demand excitement, doctor, expansion!

The chiming of a clock.

Narrator: It was time for my lunch break. "Calm down, my dear Lele, calm down," I said to my patient. "Tomorrow..."

Patient: Oh no, doctor, not now, not now that I am almost getting excited. What is the matter? Is the archaeologist tired or has his spade been blunted? Why do you start? Certainly, your psychiatry is no more no less than excavating the mind. I, too, I have dug the craters of the mind...

Doctor: With what?

Patient (ignoring the interruption): ...and pronounced them to the world as headline ruins: "Mother Runs Amok, Kills Husband and Kids," "Christmas Suicides Spiral," "Moon Worshippers Trapped in Wish Cubicles," "Jack the Reaper: TV Celebrity by Day, Pole-vaulter by Night," "Gundamentalists Seize the Day." Can't you see? I have given the world its memories. I am the memory of the world.

Doctor (slowly): You have given the world its memories? You are the memory of the world? Do you have that much faith in your newspaper headlines?

Patient: I am; therefore, the world thinks and believes and recites. When the comet of rubbles returns and our strange glints go out with its dust armada, the children of the future will think in the headlines I have left behind. They will commission great excavations and exult over my headlines. First, I will become a footnote, then an endnote, and ultimately the last word. (In a different voice): "According to Lele's *Almanac*, the world in 2000 was made up of Dead Czars and Live Pharaohs. Quod erat demonstrandum." Because I am, I will yet become.

The chiming of a clock.

Narrator: It was the clock in my mind this time. "Now, my dear man, I really think..." I began to say to my patient.

Patient: Don't you feel any tremor, doctor?

Doctor (slowly): You have given the world its memories? You are the memory of the world? Something tells me that is the key.

Patient: To what? To the year of the Ever Ever, when the world will be all windows and no doors?

Doctor: And what has the world given you?

Patient: Raw materials, plenty of seed yams. Nelson Mandela: Amandla!

Doctor: Ibrahim Gap-tooth?

Patient: Ventriloquist Africanizes the Mirage.

Doctor: George Washington?

Patient: Ropes of Sand Nationalize a Dream.

Doctor: Adolf Hitler?

Patient: Headmaster of Eugenics Hallucinates Perfection.

Doctor: Mao Tse Tung?

Patient: Great Protector Motions Great Leap Forward.

Doctor: Raw materials, eh?

Patient (crisply): I collect them all, trim the edges, feed them into the cauldron of the mind and ya-hoo, the memories of the world according to Lele. (With a chuckle): Mao Tse Tung: Chairman Wipes Posterior with Proletariat Fingers.
Doctor: Adolf Hitler?
Patient: Holocaust Monster Plays God as Satan.
Doctor: George Washington?
Patient: Patron Saint of Finger-Pointers Nabbed as a Junkie in Harlem.
Doctor: Ibrahim Gap-tooth?
Patient: King of Castle Hill Annuls the People's Mandate, Signs Own Warrant.
Doctor: Nelson Mandela?
Patient: Amandla?
Doctor: These are the memories of the world according to Lele?
Patient: Yes, some of them, privatized by me. I can't help it. And you know what, doctor? What cannot be helped perhaps should not be helped.
Doctor (slowly): What cannot be helped perhaps should not be helped. What should not be helped should not be helped, eh?

The chiming of a clock.

Narrator: The clock in my mind was still telling me that I should go to lunch, but my professional instinct was asking me to ignore it. There was something about Lele that afternoon that told me that at last we were on the verge. D.B. Lele seemed set finally to reveal himself to me, to further reveal himself to himself even. But something in him also seemed to be holding him back. It was not the time to ask the reason why.
Doctor: Come on, Lele, come on, why hold back now? Come on, man, come o-n! Bare it all to the man in the mirror. Bare it all to me.

Noise of wind, rain, and thunder as the lights dim.

Patient (dreamily): We met in the churchyard, doctor, the four of us – on a night when the elements seemed to be rebelling against God. It was the night of the first moon. We had all run into the churchyard seeking shelter and, there, we found it – in contemplations of the Star of Nubia, the lost star of the Hallelujah Enlightenment. We all had our different needs. Farida was having an ongoing battle with her co-wife. Adaeze was searching for a missing stepdaughter. Abdallah was tormented by the shattering of dreams his late mother had propped up for him. I was striving to peel the layers of reality. All of us were one continent, a continent awash with wasting lives and dreams.

Lights brighten.

Doctor (sharply): Four people a continent?
Patient: We na Africa: Africa na we. We Africa. Africa We. The two na the same. We swore great oaths that night and we began to celebrate the Communion of Redemption. We hoped to project our needs on the screen of the cosmos and have them fulfilled, separately and collectively. We hoped to illuminate the Star of Nubia once more and to become one with it. Our hopes were the questions, our Communion the sacrifice. We were the Graveyard Collective. The answer, the complete revelation, was to come in three bursts of thunder, three!
Doctor: Has the Communion a form, a rhythm?
Patient: Of course. Farida always comes first, from the periphery of need into the center of sacrifice. And the wind is always our primal witness, always.

The rush of the wind as the lights dim.

Farida (intones, as she descends from the auditorium, dressed in a white wrapper and red beads, and carrying a bowl of fire): The Star of Nubia is the primal priest of the cosmos.
Echo: Primal priest of the cosmos.
Farida: And I am one of its inner rays.

Echo: Inner rays.
Farida: Hallelujah!
Echo: Hallelujah!
Farida (sings mellifluously):

        Ukonwa, ka m kara gi
        Inine
        Nwunye di m di njo
        Inine
        Eje m ekuru mmiri nge enye nwa
        Inine
        O si m kwuo ya ugwo mmiri, mmiri nwa
        Inine
        Asi m echuo m Ogba osi m echuna Ogba
        Inine
        Asi m echuo m Imo osi m echuna Imo
        Inine
        Mmiri gini?
        Inine
        Eze Ogba
        Inine
        Mmiri suru wam wam laa n' enigwe
        Inine
        Mmiri kelu amuma k'onwa n'eti
        Inine
        Ewu-o nne nwa ndo
        Inine
        Do-o do-o
        Ini-n-e.

She kneels to the east of the totem on the fore part of the other side of the stage, her bowl of fire placed in front of her. Lights brighten on the other side.

Patient (ecstatically): O Farida, what ears can resist her voice? O Farida, angel of the star-spangled horizon.

Doctor: Why does she always come first?
Patient: She's the Nativity, the beginning of the cycle of questions. She is A Hallelujah Y.
Doctor: But she's not asking for a child or anything. She's complaining, to a barren woman, that her co-wife prevented her from fetching water for her child. What Nativity do you mean?
Patient (still enchanted): O Farida, how, like in a serial dream, I always come back to you.
Doctor: You appear to have a crush on her.
Patient: What Lele can resist a Farida, doctor? But we all swore a great oath, so I must learn again to bear my hunger like a spirit. But Farida and I are not strangers entirely. We have had several trysts in several dream-worlds.
Doctor: Does she know?
Patient: What?
Doctor: About your obsession with her.
Patient: You still don't understand, doctor. We're an entire continent of hopes and designs.
Doctor: Still, the heart wants what the heart wants, eh?
Patient (with a tinge of regret): Still and still and still, the foolish heart. But I deviate. Adaeze always comes after Farida. She is B Hallelujah Y.

The rush of the wind as the lights dim.

Adaeze (intones, descending from the auditorium, wearing a white wrapper and red beads, and carrying a bowl of fire): The Star of Nubia is the primal priest of the cosmos.
Echo: Primal priest of the cosmos.
Adaeze: And I am one of its inner rays.
Echo: Inner rays.
Adaeze: Hallelujah!
Echo: Hallelujah!
Adaeze (sings):

        Iyi ni o dodo lima

> Do do dodo lima
> Iyi ni o dodo lima
> Do do dodo lima
> Nmanu nwa Ebele ana-o
> Do do lima
> Ona-o dodo lima

She kneels facing Farida, the totem in-between, her bowl of fire placed in front of her. Lights brighten on the other side.

Patient (with a sigh): But for Farida she could have been something to hear and to see and to contemplate. Adaeze: Daughter of a King. They named her well.

Doctor: Are you sure she's got her lines right? She too comes, not asking, but lamenting, to the river, that a daughter – her stepdaughter, you said? – has passed away. What is the need that she expresses?

Patient: The metaphor is greater than the reality, doctor. And in each metaphor is an enlarging question.

Doctor: "Let there be light." There is no question in that.

Patient: The darkness was the question and the light the answer. Farida comes asking for continuity. And Abdallah comes asking for direction. Abdallah always comes after Adaeze. He is C Hallelujah Y.

The rush of the wind as the lights dim.

Abdallah (intones, descending from the auditorium, wearing a red wrapper and white beads, and carrying a stick of fire): The Star of Nubia is the primal priest of the cosmos.

Echo: Primal priest of the cosmos.

Abdallah: And I am one of its inner rays.

Echo: Inner rays.

Abdallah: Hallelujah!

Echo: Hallelujah!

Abdallah (sings):
> Nne nnem-o udu m alaputa m-o

> Udu
> Udu m ji chube iyi na mu amaro n'udu awaa
> Udu
> Obu mu solu udu k'obu mu ghalu udu naa
> Udu
> Udu m ji chube iyi udu-o-o-o
> Udu m ji chube iyi udu-o-o-o
> Anyi ga agbana ba, ewu-o
> Anyi ga agbana ba, ewu-o
> Nwunye nna m-e
> Ego nna m-e
> Anyi ga agbana ba, ewu-o

He kneels backing the auditorium, his stick of fire placed upright in front of him. Lights brighten on the other side.

Doctor (shuddering): Lord, have mercy! He has certainly been miscast!

Patient: Miscast, how?

Doctor: He comes complaining, to his mother, that his water pot is broken and he doesn't know whether to leave it or to stick with it. Mark you, he's not really expressing any need. And his singing is rather undistinguished.

Patient (with vigor): Note this carefully, doctor: it's a childhood song that he sings. It's his childhood excavated, his past addressing his present on the threshold of his future. You see, life is a cycle and the metaphor is always greater than the reality. Intervention. Continuity. Direction. These are the cardinal needs, and Farida and Adaeze and Abdallah are only three signifiers from a communal Storehouse of Memories.

Doctor: There are four inner rays. What does the fourth signify?

Patient: That's me, D Hallelujah Y.

The rush of the wind as the lights dim.

Lele (intones, coming from the backstage, wearing a red wrapper and white beads, and carrying a stick of fire): The Star of Nubia is the primal priest of the cosmos.
Echo: Primal priest of the cosmos.
Lele: And I am one of its inner rays.
Echo: Inner rays.
Lele: Hallelujah!
Echo: Hallelujah!
Lele (sings):

>Onikaluku jeje ewure
>Ewure ewure
>Onikaluku jeje aguntan
>Aguntan kpolojo
>Oluronbi jeje omore
>Omore akpon bi ekpo
>Oluronbi o join join
>Iroko join join

He kneels facing the auditorium, his stick of fire placed upright in front of him. Lights go out. When the lights are restored, the four are no longer on stage. Lele is back on the couch. The bowls, sticks of fire, and the totem remain on stage.

Doctor: Quite interesting, your singing. Very interesting. Farida plus Abdallah minus Adaeze, that's the simple equation.
Patient (with a laugh): That's not bad. (Dreamily) O Farida!
Doctor (with a laugh): Farida, eh? But you're playing a redundant role, my man. You come narrating the tale of a woman. She pledged her child while the rest of the world was pledging goats and rams. A fool of a woman, sure, but how does her foolishness fit into the communion of needs seeking a redemptive sign in metaphors of thunder?
Patient: I come asking, counseling, pragmatism.
Doctor (amazed): You, counseling pragmatism? Certainly, you too have been miscast. Pragmatism is the straitjacket of the conservative, the credo of coup-plotters and kleptocrats. Redemption comes in

heroic leaps of the imagination. Redemption comes in great bursts of the will to be and to do and to be and to do over and over again.
Patient: The metaphor is greater than...
Doctor: The great D. B. Lele now taking refuge behind travel-worn expressions, eh? Come on, man, get back into character. Hallelujah?
Patient: Hallelujah!
Doctor: What next? We have witnessed the four rays converge from different corners of need around the emblem of the Star of Nubia. That is what we have witnessed, right? So, does the revelation come?
Patient (sadly): It does, doctor, but it's never complete.

Two bursts of thunder, in separate blasts.

Patient (counting): One...two...Oh, just one more, just one more to make it three in all and the revelation will be complete. Night after night, I have lain awake, doctor, tormented by this singular absence – until, finally, finally, my torments and my nightmares have led me to you. Why, oh why, is the revelation never complete and therefore never effective? Just one more, katabo-o-o-o-m, but it never comes.
Doctor: There is a magic in numbers?
Patient: Every each one. One is solitude. Me and I.
Doctor: Two?
Patient: Companionship. We the twins.
Doctor: Three?
Patient: Epiphany. Anointment.
Doctor: Four?
Patient: Harmony. All roads disperse, all roads converge.
Doctor: Five
Patient: Shine. The chefs are all ready.
Doctor: Six?
Patient: Sickle. Short lived your comrades.
Doctor: Seven?
Patient: Victory. The triumphal entry.
Doctor: Eight?
Patient (with a sigh): Freight. Farida on my mind.

Doctor: Nine?
Patient: Questions. Which is the freedom road?
Doctor: Ten?
Patient: Diffusion. The icons of the tribe become those of the world.
Doctor: Three: epiphany, seven: victory. So, why settle for three instead of seven?
Patient: The third before the seventh, doctor, the third before! Every Complete Revelation carries in its genes the seeds of victory. Every Complete Revelation is a victory in the wings. I am a continent on the slaughter slab. I am the incomplete revelation: D Hallelujah Y.
Doctor: And what is the Complete Revelation?
Patient: Hallelujah! No prefix, no suffix.
Doctor: And what is the signal chant of victory?
Patient (in a chant): Hallelujah! Hallelujah! Hallelujah!
Doctor: There is no doubt about it. You are the great privatizer. Tell me: where did you finally piece it all together? Cities have a certain magic in them too, you know.
Patient: Of course, of course. Lagos: City of Frenzy.
Doctor: Cairo?
Patient: Alabaster of the Nativity. (With a chuckle): The pharaohs are nice in stone.
Doctor: Paris?
Patient: Cest Paris! Cest Paris!
Doctor: London?
Patient (in a falsetto): It's nice knowing you, honey, but I don't do exiles.
Doctor: New York?
Patient: Vanity upon vanity, all is vanity.
Doctor: You agree that cities have a certain magic in them too?
Patient: Every each thing, doctor, every each thing.
Narrator: Perhaps that was the point I became both the spade and the sand, the priest as well as the sacrifice. I wanted to help my patient to rise up to his other self. And yes, yes, I must admit it, I couldn't resist the temptation of using him in my experiments. So, I said to him:

Every Communion of Redemption is a return to the future, do you believe that?
Patient: Return to the future, how?
Doctor: You take a thing, a person – anything! – as it is and you stretch, s-t-r-e-t-c-h, it beyond its parenthesis, what do you think you are doing? You are extending, e-x-t-e-n-d-i-n-g, that thing or person, returning it, to the future – reinventing it. Why does your Communion merely point when Africa is crying to be reinvented? What we must do is to reinvent your memories.
Patient (rather puzzled): How can memories be reinvented? How can you reinvent the past, doctor? Are you sure I'm not in your place and you in mine?
Doctor: Perhaps. Quote: "Certainty is not of this world." Unquote. D. B. Lele himself. Remember? The journey we have to make is simple: we begin in the past, in your memory, where all things terminate, and we end in the future, in your projection, where all things originate. Quote: "The metaphor is greater than the reality." Unquote. D. B. Lele himself. I will be the Fifth Inner Ray.
Patient: But there are only four directions – west, east, north and south.
Doctor: We will create a fifth and we shall call it *wenst* – a direction without frontiers, without fixed aspects. You see, the first law of extraordinary movement is to reinvent geography.
Patient: And after that?
Doctor: The sound of the homeland, the sound of A-f-r-i-c-a!

Celebrative, drum-based song (or music) as lights further brighten, then dim and return to normal.

Doctor: Africa is the navel of the earth.
Echo: Navel of the earth.
Doctor: And I am one of its missing links.
Echo: Missing links.
Doctor: Mena!
Echo: Mena!

Patient: Mena! What does it mean? Some kind of spirit-calling mumbo-jumbo?

Doctor: Mena is "Amen" made new. Quote. "Why should things, all things, not be reinvented beyond their common dimensions?" Unquote. D. B. Lele himself. Now, as one, we will convoke around the emblem of the Star of Nubia.

Patient: Farida is east, Adaeze is west, Abdallah is south, and I am north. In which direction is wenst?

Doctor: You see, you've got your poles wrong. How can you be north and Abdallah south when your hunger for Farida is eating you up? Farida will be south, you north, Abdallah east, and Adaeze west. I will crown the circle when I drop from the sky.

Patient: Drop from the sky?

Doctor: We must reach for the signified Star of Nubia. We must reach for that reality which empowers the metaphor. We will reach for the sky! Now, open the gates of your memory.

Patient (slowly): Speak again, memory.

Doctor (slowly): Speak ahead, memory.

Lights come on dimly, on the other side of the stage. The bowls and sticks of fire have been removed. The patient and the doctor are standing beside the totem, wearing a red wrapper and white beads and a red-white wrapper and white-red beads respectively. Celebrative, drum-based music as lights further brighten, then dim and go out.

Doctor and **Patient:** Africa is the navel of the earth.

Echo: Navel of the earth.

Doctor and **Patient:** And we are its missing links.

Echo: Missing links.

Doctor and **Patient:** Mena!

Echo: Mena.

Doctor and **Patient:** Nkosi Sikelel' iAfrika.

Patient: Nkosi Sikelel' iAfrika: God bless Hallelujah Y. Can't we be more specific than that?

Doctor: Perhaps. But ours must be a song of power, not another whine from void into void.
Patient (with spirit): Let Farida sing it. What ears can resist the natalitial voice of the Niger?
Farida (sings, descending from the auditorium, dressed as before, carrying a bowl of fire):

>	Nwunye di m n'ako m onu n'uwa-e
>	O nwunye di m n'ako m onu n'uwa-e
>	Olisa nye m nwa
>	Obulu n'iga enye m nwa
>	K'inye mie na gbo-o

She kneels backing the auditorium, her bowl placed in front of her.

Patient (wonderingly): But that's a demand, not a request. Whose is the power?
Doctor: There is power in power. She doesn't want to wait forever. Her request is simple: "Give me a child quickly, O God, if you will." The will is everything.
Patient: One more song to make it three? Three is the number, three!
Doctor: Yes, a song for three – for you, Abdallah and Adaeze. It's a song without words.
Patient: How does one sing a song without words?
Doctor: Farida came dancing her demand. So it should be. You and Abdallah and Adaeze will come in slow but deathless strides dancing a wordless song of power.
Patient: Saying what?
Doctor: Saying everything potent that has been said and everything potent that has not been said. So it should be. Mena?
Patient: Mena!

Adaeze and Abdallah come from the auditorium and Lele, from the direction of the backstage, silently doing a stylized dance, the men carrying a stick of fire each and the woman a bowl of fire. Each kneels before the totem accordingly. A cock crows in the background.

Patient: We are here, E Hallelujah Y. We have come from the periphery to the center. Our sticks and bowl of fire are at last placed at the base of the emblem of the Star of Nubia. What next?

Doctor: Time now for the leap of power. Come on, people, time to form a foothold with your offertory palms to prop the crown of power.

The four rise and form a foothold.

   Now, time for the leap.

Leaps upward, aided by the foothold, on top of the totem.

   And now, together, people, together!

All Five: Nkosi Sikelel' iAfrika!

Three bursts of thunder, in separate blasts.

Patient (counting): One...two...THREE! AT LAST, at l-a-s-t, the Complete Revelation. Hallelujah!

Doctor:
Descends
   Now, together, people, together!

All Five: H-a-l-l-e-l-u-j-a-h!

Three bursts of thunder, in separate blasts.

Patient (counting): One... two... three. Six in all. More by three. What now?

Lights go out. When the lights are restored, in the doctor's office, only the Patient and Doctor are on stage. The Patient is back on the couch, the Doctor in his chair, both dressed as they were at the beginning.

Doctor (contemplatively): Even thunder can break. And then it must be reinvented.

Patient (in a chant): Three times three: nine. Three minus three: zero. Three divide three: one. Three plus three: six. More, less, less, more. Never exact.

Doctor: There is a fifth option.
Patient: What?
Doctor: Three three is three; three three is three accented. "Dreams are not enough," repeats the thunder. Three three is the thunder of action.
Patient: "All peaks begin on the peaks of dreams." That is what the thunder will say. Dreams are...
Doctor (emphatically): STARTERS!
Patient (emphatically): SUPREME!
Doctor: Nkosi Sikelel' iAfrika. Come on, people, a-l-l together, all t-o-g-e-t-h-e-r!
Audience: Nkosi Sikelel' iAfrika.

Bursts of thunder.

Doctor: Again, people, a-l-l together, all t-o-g-e-t-h-e-r!
Audience: Nkosi Sikelel' iAfrika.

Bursts of thunder.

Blackout.

When the lights are restored, the doctor is alone in his consulting room with a postcard in his hands.

Narrator: D.B. Lele, BSc Honors, MSc, MPhil, Journalist Sui Generis, the Big Noise Himself, what a character! We parted without an agreement. But we parted on very good terms, and he left in better spirits than the day he burst into my office. Three months passed. I didn't hear from him or about him. Still, I kept his file open. I kept it open until this morning when I finally received a postcard from him, a postcard with only one sentence.
Lele's voice: In the final analysis, most answers are questions reinvented. Hallelujah?

Narrator: The last bit was a signature, an old one in a new form, and a question – a question to which I had only one answer (with zeal): Hallelujah!

Blackout.

———

Lagos, Nigeria
January 1995

www.ingramcontent.com/pod-product-compliance
Lightning Source LLC
LaVergne TN
LVHW041643070526
838199LV00053B/3543